Beautiful
IRELAND

Beautiful
IRELAND

A Celebration of Ireland's People and Places

Mary Fitzgerald

John Hinde
ORIGINAL

Published by
John Hinde Ltd.,
Dublin, Ireland.

DEDICATION

for Peggy and George Whalley
and Kay and John Devine
with my love

5147
This edition published in 2001 by John Hinde

Produced by Quadrillion Publishing Limited
ISBN 1-901123-28-6

Printed in Italy
by EUROLITHO SpA - Cesano Boscone (MI)

Editor: Jane Alexander
Design: Mik Martin and Louise Clements
Original design concept: Thomas Keene
Design Manager: Justina Leitão
Photography by John Hinde Ltd

The author and publishers would like to
thank Richard Killeen for providing additional
text and Don Sutton International for the
photographs on pages 133 top, 138 bottom,
139, 141 and Christopher Hill for the
photographs on pages 104 top, 105, 121,
126 all, 128, 129 both, 131, 132, 133
bottom, 134 left, 135 right, 136, 140

Endpapers: Waterford at night.
Half title: Desmond Castle, Adare.
Title page: part of the Ring of Beara.

This page:
Main pic: the Round Tower at Glendalough.
Right, from top: Little Skellig.
Dun Aengusa fort, in the Aran Islands.
The Carrick-a-rede rope bridge.
Blarney Castle.

CONTENTS

INTRODUCTION

By no stretch of the imagination is Ireland large: it is possible to drive from Co. Kerry in the extreme west across the country to Dublin, on the east coast, in an afternoon. But what an afternoon! For though it may be small, this land is rare in its wondrous variety. It doesn't feel small, such is the wealth of different sights and experiences on offer travelling through it. Take that route from Kerry to Dublin, for example. Start on the approach to Killarney, the heart of Kerry's world-renowned mountain scenery, and pass the county's famed lakes and the desmense of Muckross House with jaunting cars aplenty along the way. As you continue through Killarney and on towards bustling Tralee, over your shoulder is one of the most memorable sights of the West – the silhouette of MacGillycuddy's Reeks clear, Killarney nestling below.

Yet just a few kilometres later, beyond Tralee and heading north to the Shannon estuary the country runs flat, the sky seems to get larger, and the beaches sweep out at Ballybunion into glorious arcs of sand beside imposing cliffs. Swinging left one travels beside the wide Shannon, the most majestic of Ireland's rivers, as the road follows the mighty waterway into the heart of Limerick. Here, as in every Irish town of note, there is the old side by side with the new, living history around every corner.

Out from Limerick, the Dublin road is flanked on the left by the Galtée Mountains, their fine shape lending a sheltered feel to the rich, rolling farmland of Tipperary and Limerick at their feet. Then, not long after, you cross the great expanse of the Curragh at Kildare, an ancient place where the spring of thoroughbreds across the turf remains a delight. Soon the blue swathes of the Wicklow Mountains can be seen in the distance, sheltering Dublin, silvered by the Liffey, and home, like much of Ireland, to many more than just those fortunate enough to live there. In all, a various land, a magical one, and all in an afternoon!

In short, a rich and rare land, just waiting to be explored!

Left: boats tethered invitingly near Ross Castle.

LEINSTER

Leinster's variety ranges from the peacefulness of the
Wicklow hills to the buzz of the country's capital.

Below: Dublin's famous eighteenth-century Custom's House and the bracingly modern Financial Services Centre stand side by side on the banks of the Liffey, symbols of Dublin's business life past and present.

Dublin

Dublin lies beside the Irish Sea a little to the north of the Wicklow Mountains. The capital city of the Republic of Ireland, it first came into existence as a Viking trading centre a thousand years ago. Today the city still has as its centre the River Liffey, famed in poetry and prose, which divides Dublin into north and south sides. There is an appreciable difference in atmosphere between the two sections, recognized by Dubliners and perceivable by visitors.

Dublin is various; this is part of its charm. Side by side, almost, one can enjoy the dignified grounds of Trinity College and the bustling shops in Grafton Street and O'Connell Street, the famous squares of Georgian Dublin and the cries and colours of street markets. Temple Bar's cool galleries and this youthful area's gaudily painted shops contast with the raffish, crowded pubs all over the city and the serene town parks at its centre.

To the northwest of the city is the broad sweep of Europe's largest city park, Phoenix Park, while not far from the illustrious quayside buildings is the sea: a walk on Bull Island strand or along the harbour wall to Dublin's little red lighthouse gives a new perspective on the city. To the south of the city, the Wicklow mountains are less than an hour's drive from the centre. There one can look down on the complete panorama from high in the hills, a view that is especially beautiful at night.

Previous pages: the Great Sugarloaf Mountain, Co. Wicklow.

Above left: Molly Malone's statue at the foot of Grafton Street. The song 'Cockles and Mussels' immortalises the street sellers who walked the city in former times.

Below: O'Connell Street, Dublin's main shopping thoroughfare, is lined with statues of famous Irishmen, including Daniel O'Connell.

Right: Davy Byrnes, the pub portrayed by James Joyce in his great novel *Ulysses*, is as friendly now as it was considered to be then.

Below: graffiti as an art form in Temple Bar.

Below right: O'Connell's pub in Dublin displays a typically cheerful front.

Above: shoppers, students and tourists mingle in Temple Bar. Here one can find art studios, cinemas, galleries, restaurants and alternative shops, impromptu street markets and buskers galore.

Left: O'Donoghue's, one of Dublin's most famous pubs, is renowned for traditional Irish music.

Arguably one of the most famous Dublin sights is the 'most beautiful book in the world', the Book of Kells, a superbly illuminated copy of the Gospels that dates from *c.* 800. This treasured volume is held as part of Trinity College's extensive and venerable Old Library, the highlight of which is the 'Long Room', a serene, lofty space, well lit and unforgettable in its Classical order and subdued decoration.

Trinity College was founded in 1592 by Queen Elizabeth I of England. For centuries the university only received Protestants, while Catholics viewed it with suspicion; today, however, its elegant campus is open to all, and in scholarly terms it ranks alongside Oxford and Cambridge.

Some of the most impressive buildings in the capital are connected with the Irish government. Leinster House on Kildare Street, formerly the town mansion of the Dukes of Leinster, is the seat of the two houses of the country's national parliament, the House of Representatives, known as the Dáil (pronounced 'doyle'), and the Senate. The imposing Government Buildings on Merrion Street once housed the Royal College of Science.

Above: Parliament Square of Trinity College. Famous alumni of the college include the writers Jonathan Swift, Oliver Goldsmith, Oscar Wilde and Samuel Beckett.

Right: Merrion Street's Government Buildings.

GEORGIAN DUBLIN

Georgian Dublin is epitomised by its doors. The seemingly infinite variations upon a certain distinctive design (see these pages) are rumoured to have arisen in order that their original owners could distinguish their own door from others when they returned inebriated. Formerly, as in Georgian England, it was the habit to paint all front doors black, but the uniformity of the terraced houses meant that they appeared all the same to those 'slightly the worse for wear'.

Now the tall terraces of such as Merrion Square are rarely private houses in their entirety: the lower rooms are rented to serve as discreetly distinguished offices for professionals such as solicitors, doctors and dentists. Only the top rooms are likely to be used as flats, but, unsurprisingly, these remain highly desirable: a number of well-preserved Georgian streets, particularly on the south side of the city, are the 'best' addresses in town.

Above: terraced houses four storeys high in Fitzwilliam Square, Dublin's smallest and best-preserved Georgian square. Part of its beauty lies in a secluded, private central park.
Right: a stern face, a classic piece of Georgian door furniture to be seen all around the city.

Wicklow

They call County Wicklow the garden of Ireland and it's not hard to see why. The county is shielded to the north, west and south by the beautiful Wicklow Mountains and fringed by the sea to the east, and its rural attractions are very well known. The mountains beckon walkers, being of comparatively gentle incline: there are superb waterfalls necklacing the glens, such as that at Glenmacnass, and magical loughs, such as Lough Tay, Lough Dan and the Lower and Upper lakes at Glendalough, set like jewels in the folds of the hills. Yet for all their popularity, the mountains remain aloof and lonely: it is still possible to drive the old Military Road from north to south and see not a soul: just sheep and stillness, or wild wind and weather.

In recent times the beauty of the county has reached a wider audience since the Wicklow village of Avoca doubles as the eponymous village in the popular television series *Ballykissangel*. Avoca was famed previously as the birthplace of the Irish politician Charles Stewart Parnell: today it welcomes visitors eager to see the locations made famous in the series. Wicklow is also renowned for some of the finest beaches on Ireland's east coast. Brittas Bay, the enticingly named Silver Strand, and Jack's Hole are superb stretches of white sand: out of season one may have them all to oneself, although they are not a well-kept secret: hundreds arrive from the city to enjoy them on summer days. Equally popular is the northerly resort of Bray. Its position at the end of the 'Dart', Dublin's commuter railway, means that it is accessible to daytrippers in under an hour, and many come to enjoy its superb promenade, its well-kept beach and its wealth of Victorian architecture.

Above: the lake at Powerscourt Gardens, a mile from Enniskerry. The gardens were originally laid out in the eighteenth century, but radically redesigned during the nineteenth.

Right: Mount Usher Gardens, near Ashford. These beautiful grounds were laid out in the nineteenth century by the Walpole family, and contain some rare and exotic plants.

Below: silver sand at Brittas Bay, protected by sand dunes. Over a third of Wicklow's coastline is fringed with such beaches.

Above: serene Lough Tay is midnight blue in summer, a chilling black in winter weather.

Left: Fitzgerald's pub, Avoca, a site of much drama in the television series *Ballykissangel*.

Far left: the top of the tremendous waterfall of the Glenmacnass River, beautifully situated at the head of the valley. Water tumbles here over a sheer drop from a height of eighty metres (262 feet).

Kildare

L ike the racing town of Newmarket in England, Kildare town lies close to a heath that is ideal for testing thoroughbreds. Known as the Curragh, this is the largest commonage in the country, holding not only the biggest army camp in Ireland but also its most famous racecourse too. The Irish Derby is run here each June. Kildare is recognised as the home of Ireland's National Stud. Here some of the finest bloodstock in the world are bred and reared: Ireland enjoys an international reputation for the quality of her racehorses, and breeding them is one of the country's major industries.

The stud itself was founded by an eccentric English colonel. He arranged the buildings, the training, purchases and sale of his horses with reference to astrology, consulting the individual horoscopes of the animals to determine his decisions. He was remarkably successful, winning most of the major Irish races at the turn of the century. He was also passionate about horticulture, and commissioned a team of Japanese gardeners to create a truly superb garden, bringing trees and shrubs direct from Japan. In 1916 the colonel gave both the stud and the gardens to the British Crown, who passed them on to the Irish government in 1943.

Below: White's Castle, built *c.* 1500 to defend the bridge in Athy.

Above: Trim Castle, the largest Anglo-Norman castle in Ireland, boasts not only a twelfth-century keep, but also a fine set of curtain walls and connecting towers, sally-ports and a barbican. It was used as a location in the film *Braveheart*.

Right: the entrance to the passage grave at Newgrange, an extraordinary feat of Neolithic architecture and astronomical calculation.

Meath

The county of Meath, to the north of Dublin, is perhaps best known for the greatest passage grave in Neolithic Europe, at Newgrange in the Boyne valley, which dates from between 2800 and 2400 B.C. By the entrance is the famous threshold stone, carved with spirals, diamonds and circles. The passage leads to an impressive tomb chamber. Due to sophisticated astronomical calculations, the length of the long passage and the entrance of the tomb itself are only touched by daylight in their entirety during the winter equinox on 21 December.

Meath is also thought to be the original home of the Book of Kells, the superbly illuminated manuscript of the Gospels that now resides in Trinity College, Dublin. A facsimile is on show in St Columba's Church, Kells. Kells was a thriving early Christian centre of learning between the eighth and tenth centuries. It is known that the Book of Kells belonged to this monastery, although it is not certain if it was actually produced there.

Also of interest in Meath is the Hill of Tara, famous as the base for the High Kings of Ireland but actually an Iron Age Celtic hill fort and a Neolithic passage grave. The hill offers superb views of the surrounding countryside.

Above and above left: the main street and pretty town houses in Trim, a town that in medieval times was the centre of a great pilgrimage to the Augustinian abbey's statue of the Blessed Virgin Mary. All that now remains of the abbey is a broken tower.

Below left: the church on the Hill of Tara lit by evening light. The church boasts both medieval and twentieth-century stained glass, while the churchyard contains the remains of a Bronze Age standing stone.

Above: Tynan's Bridge House Bar, one of the most famous and beloved pubs in Kilkenny city, was once a pharmacy and a grocer's. Visitors can still see the accoutrements of these former uses in the bar, all lit by the soft glow of old-fashioned gas lamps.

Right: Kilkenny city is built on limestone, which polishes to a shining black. Hence it has been known for centuries as the Marble City, a name reflected in this pub.

Kilkenny

The Anglo-Norman invaders of Kilkenny in the thirteenth century made a dramatic difference to the county that is still visible today. Particularly notable are the numerous abbeys built around this time, such as Duiske, in Graiguenamanagh, formerly the largest Cistercian abbey in Ireland, and Jerpoint, near Thomastown. Jerpoint has been partially restored and its almost complete buildings are fascinating; the figure carvings in the cloister are especially noteworthy.

The Anglo-Normans were also responsible for the grand castles that dominate the county. The most memorable of these is probably Kilkenny Castle, for all that it was largely rebuilt in the nineteenth century. Commanding the River Nore and Kilkenny city, the castle was the seat of the county's most influential family, the Butlers. The Butler family descended from the twelfth-century Anglo-Norman knight Theobald Fitzwalter, who accompanied Henry II to Ireland in 1171; he was made Chief Butler in Ireland and Earl of Ormond, hence the family name.

Across Kilkenny city from the castle, in Irishtown, stands the serene St Canice's Cathedral, largely destroyed by Cromwell but later lovingly rebuilt. One of the finest restored churches in Ireland, it is noted for its beautiful medieval tomb monuments and its round tower in the churchyard.

Above: a Kilkenny pub sign. Kilkenny Irish beer is available throughout the country.

Below left: a colourful pub in Kilkenny city. Kilkenny is known for the number and quality of its hostelries, some of which are found in evocative old buildings.

Right: a fountain plays in the sunlight before the castellated front of Kilkenny Castle. A portion of the palatial grounds of the castle was given to the people of Kilkenny in 1967; today both the grounds and the castle itself are open to visitors. On a fine day, the view from the battlements as the county stretches before one is unsurpassed anywhere in the city.

Left: the River Nore at Thomastown. A small market town established by the Normans, Thomastown was once walled and boasted a sizeable castle. No longer of such importance, nevertheless it can still claim an old bridge and a defence tower by the river, and it is set among some of the loveliest countryside in the county.

Below: the arch-supported tower of Jerpoint Abbey, near Thomastown. This Cistercian monastery is in a very good state of repair. Partially rebuilt in the 1950s, Jerpoint is thought to have been founded in 1180 by Donal MacGillapatrick. The monastery's first abbot, Felix O'Dullany, was also the founder of Kilkenny city's St Canice's Cathedral.

Wexford

The town of Wexford existed as a settlement on the estuary of the River Slaney for at least two thousand years, but it came into its own as a trading port in the hands of the Vikings just over a thousand years ago. Today it is the county town of Wexford, and its charmingly narrow streets are a focus for manufacturing and marketing. There are some sites of historical interest: one of the five fortified gates built by the Normans still exists, as do relics of the former walls, while one can also see the remains of both a fine abbey, Selskar Abbey (the Abbey of the Holy Sepulchre), and a priory of the Knights Hospitallers, St Mary's.

Although not a large town, Wexford was the birthplace of a surprising number of famous people. The great Arctic explorer and discoverer of the Northwest Passage, Sir Robert J. McClure, hails from Wexford, as do Oscar Wilde's remarkable mother, the colourful writer and patriot known as 'Speranza', and the nineteenth-century Irish landscape painter Francis Danby. Music lovers all over Ireland also think of Wexford as the centre of the Wexford Art and Music Festival, better known as the Opera Festival, which takes place (despite the lack of an opera house) every autumn.

JOHNSTOWN CASTLE

Beautifully set in landscaped grounds and equally beautifully maintained, Johnstown Castle was built in the nineteenth century to a design by Daniel Robertson which incorporated a remaining thirteenth-century tower. This had been part of a stronghold of the Esmondes and Fitzgerald families that was otherwise destroyed by Cromwell before he attacked Wexford in 1649. The castle was given to the state in 1944 and today houses a fine agricultural museum and an agricultural institute, as well as featuring a working farm in the environs. The elegant grounds, lakes and gardens are all open to the public.

Carlow

Ireland's second smallest county, Carlow was the site of many a dramatic battle during the Middle Ages, as the English king Richard II sought to defeat his scourge, the fourteenth-century warrior chieftain, Art Óg Mac Murrough. The rule of the English Crown in Ireland then centred on the Pale, an area of territory around Dublin that included parts of Kildare and Wicklow. Carlow stood on the edge of the Pale and so was strategically very important. Like its southerly sister, Kilkenny, it is blessed with rich agricultural land, mostly undulating or flat, but in the south, forming the border with Wexford, lie the mountains of the Blackstairs range, dominated by Mount Leinster.

At the extreme northwestern edge of the county, Carlow town, the county town, stands at an important crossing on the River Barrow. Not surprisingly, it is centred around an Anglo-Norman castle, now ruined but for the two surviving drum towers and their connecting wall. During the 1798 uprising, over 400 insurgents were ambushed and killed in a pitched battle in the town. A mass grave in a nearby gravel pit is marked with a memorial.

The River Barrow offers some of the country's finest river cruising, and Carlow today is a noted boating centre. The town also boasts one of the most popular golf courses in Ireland, which, because of its dry, sandy soil, is playable all year round. Just outside the town, at Browne's Hill, is a magnificent Neolithic dolmen. Its capstone, which weighs one hundred tons, is the largest in the land.

Laois

The midland county of Laois (pronounced 'Leesh') is mostly limestone plain and the landscape is generally not dramatic, tending towards woodland, fields and bog. However, this means that what hills there are afford superb views. In the east lie a striking range of isolated, circular outcrops known as 'hums', and to the west are the Slieve Bloom Mountains. The latter do not rise to any great height, but amid them lie over twenty glens of considerable charm and tranquillity.

The county town is Portlaoise (originally known as Maryborough), which has some splendid public buildings, including a particularly fine courthouse built by a pupil of the celebrated architect Gandon. This English plantation town was established in the sixteenth century around a castle, which was later virtually demolished by Cromwell.

In the east of the county lies the Rock of Dunamase, possibly Laois' most famous site. This is one of several 'hums' that were used as natural sites for Celtic forts and it is very ancient, holding the distinction of having been recorded by Ptolemy. It is surmounted by the remains of a castle that once belonged to Dermot Mac Murrough, King of Leinster.

Below: the Rock of Dunamase, a steep outcrop over sixty metres (197 feet) high. On the highest point once stood the keep of a complex medieval fortress, now a ruin. The view from the rock over the surrounding countryside is unforgettable.

Offaly

Offaly is largely flat and boggy; only the Slieve Bloom Mountains that the county shares with its neighbour Laois is a region of any particular height. Indeed, much of Offaly is encompassed by the Bog of Allan, whose rich peat harvest has contributed substantially to this midland county's economy. In former times the Grand Canal was also a source of wealth. This bisects the centre of the county, joining the River Liffey and Dublin to the River Shannon on the border with Galway. During the canal's heyday in the late eighteenth and early nineteenth centuries this waterway was busy with both trade and passenger barges: in an era when travelling by road was hazardous and uncomfortable, gliding along a canal was an attractive alternative. Canal hotels like the Presbytery in Tullamore's Canal Harbour appeared in key towns en route, but canal travel was soon superseded by rail. The Grand Canal remains in use and many a visitor arrives in Offaly via this beautiful waterway.

Offaly's largest town, Tullamore, is probably best known to the rest of the world as the home of a particularly fine liqueur whiskey known as 'Irish Mist'. As a small village, it was all but destroyed by fire in 1785; the resulting rebuilding was on a much grander scale and a number of lovely Georgian houses remain in the town today.

By far Offaly's biggest tourist attraction is Clonmacnoise. This early monastic site was second only to Armagh in Northern Ireland in religious importance. It produced unsurpassed works of art, such as the Cross of Cong, now in the National Museum in Dublin, and numerous superbly carved high crosses. It was founded in the sixth century by St Ciaran. Its position on the River Shannon ensured a steady supply of monks and its fame grew until it became more a monastic city than merely a monastery. It was ruined by the English in 1552: the principal remains today are eight churches, a cathedral and two round towers.

Left: sunset silhouettes the magnificent round tower at Clonmacnoise, an important monastic settlement whose ruins lie on the banks of the River Shannon in Co. Offaly.

Westmeath and Longford

The county of Westmeath is an angler's paradise, particularly for those with a penchant for catching trout, or bream, rudd and pike. The county's four major fishing lakes, Loughs Lene, Owel, Derravaragh and Ennell, lie close to the county town of Mullingar, while numerous smaller lakes are found in the drumlin country in the north. (Drumlins are low, undulating hills which have their own charm when interspersed with lakes.) Nearly all of them offer superb fishing. The Royal Canal once ran right across Westmeath and beyond to the Shannon; today efforts are being made to open it up west of Mullingar. The towpath has been cleared from Dublin to Mullingar, and offers tranquil walks, laced with dragonflies and dog roses in season.

To the northwest of Westmeath, County Longford is bordered in the west by Ireland's longest river, the Shannon, which widens into Lough Ree. This sizeable lough is dotted with islands: one, the aptly named Saint's Island (now joined to the mainland), has a restored Augustinian monastery which flourished in the fourteenth century; another, Inchleraun, is associated with the legendary warrior queen, Maeve. The county town of Longford boasts pleasingly wide streets, the remains of a seventeenth-century castle and a fine courthouse. Here too can be found the works of the county's major authors: dramatist Oliver Goldsmith, novelist Maria Edgeworth, and the poet Padraic Colum.

Below: St Mel's Cathedral in Longford town was built in the nineteenth-century. Today it also contains an ecclesiastical museum.

Below: rowing boats
on Lough Ennell,
Co. Westmeath, a lake in
the north of the county
which is known for its
fine sailing.

Louth

Louth is the smallest county in Ireland. Situated on the border with Northern Ireland and facing the Irish Sea to the east, it provides considerable scenic variety, despite its size. The coastline offers a number of tempting sandy beaches, and the mountains of the Cooley Peninsula in the north. Tours of this area afford fine views of the high Mountains of Mourne, whose peaks lie across Carlingford Lough in Co. Derry.

The two main towns of Louth are Dundalk in the north and Drogheda in the extreme south. Dundalk, a sea port on Dundalk Bay and on the main Dublin to Belfast road, is Anglo-Norman in origin, but the town takes its name from the Irish Dun Dealgan, a prehistoric fort. Evidently people have lived here for many thousands of years. Today the town is a manufacturing centre, and contains a number of old churches.

Drogheda, near the mouth of the River Boyne, ranked in importance with Dublin, Waterford and Kilkenny as one of the four staple towns of Ireland in the Middle Ages. Cromwell captured it in 1649, and virtually everybody in the town, regardless of age or sex, was killed, some 2000 people. Cromwell deemed it 'a righteous judgement of God'. The massacre is remembered today as the height of his barbarity in conquering Ireland. Drogheda lies just three miles from another significant site in Irish history, where the Battle of the Boyne took place in 1690. This victory for Protestant forces under Prince William of Orange ('King Billy') over the Catholic English king, James II, is still commemorated in Northern Ireland each July by Protestant parades.

Far left: the awe-inspiring Muiredach's Cross at Monasterboice, one of two superb high crosses at this site of a former Christian community founded by St Boethius. Two small churches and a ninth-century round tower, sadly missing its roof, may also be seen at the site.

Left: Drogheda on the River Boyne. The embalmed head of Saint Oliver Plunkett (1628–81) can be seen in St Peter's Church. The Catholic archbishop was hanged, drawn and quartered for his part in the 'Popish Plot' and canonised in 1975.

MUNSTER

The beauties of Munster, Ireland's southwestern
province, are renowned throughout the world.

Tipperary

Tipperary, Ireland's largest inland county, is very beautiful, not least because of the several ranges of mountains on its borders. The Galtees in the southwest, the Silvermines in the north of the county, the Slieveardagh Hills in the east and the Knockmealdown Mountains in the extreme south each have their own particular character and cast a special atmosphere over the countryside they dominate. The Galtees are the highest of these ranges, reaching 1000 metres (3280 feet) at the summit of Galtymore.

Two major rivers flow through the county, the Shannon in the northwest and the Suir in the centre and southeast. The Shannon feeds Lough Derg, the largest lake on the river at some twenty-five kilometres (sixteen miles) long. Numerous islands ornament the lough, which is noted for its fishing. The Suir rises in Tipperary and winds its way down through the county's biggest towns, the delightfully named Golden, Clonmel, and Carrick-on-Suir. The latter is one of the loveliest towns in Ireland, beautifully sited and rich in historic remains, the highlight of which is the Elizabethan manor house known as Ormond Castle. Now preserved by the Office of Public Works, it is open to the public during the summer and is especially renowned for its very fine plasterwork in the Long Gallery.

Previous pages: the Blaskets and Dunmore Head, Co. Kerry.

Left: the Rock of Cashel. Seen rising from the plain as one approaches on the Dublin to Cork road, the ruins of this cathedral are magnificent in their elevated dignity and grandeur.

Below: Clonmel's turreted West Gate, one of four city gates, which was rebuilt in 1831. Parts of Clonmel's ancient walls may still be seen.

Waterford

Right: the redoubtable
grey form of Reginald's
Tower stands
incongruously among far
more modern buildings
on the Waterford
quayside. It is thought to
have been built by
Reginald the Dane in
1003 and is the oldest
tower of mortared stone
in Europe. It houses a
fine civic museum. Once
walled, like so many
Anglo-Norman towns,
Waterford has more of
its city walls remaining
than any except Derry.

Above: a busy shopping
street in Waterford, the
county town. In the
eighteenth century the
town was a leading
producer of fine lead
crystal, a tradition that
was revived in the 1950s.
Waterford Crystal is now
known the world over.

Below: a variety of boats
in Waterford Harbour,
from pleasure craft to
container ships. During
the Middle Ages,
Waterford was one of the
chief ports in all Ireland
and its commercial
importance is still very
much in evidence today.

County Waterford enjoys a long and beautiful stretch of the southeast coastline between two rivers, the Blackwater and the Suir. The Blackwater reaches the sea at Youghal, in neighbouring Cork, but for most of its length in the county, especially as it travels along at the foot of the Knockmealdown Mountains, it is Waterford's loveliest river, its wooded shores near Cappoquin being particularly fine. The Suir combines with the Barrow and the Nore to flow from the north into Waterford Harbour, a large expanse of water at the extreme southeast of the county. The coast has numerous sandy beaches, giving rise to several fine seaside resorts, such as Tramore.

Waterford was the first county to be occupied by the invading Anglo-Normans, although it owes its name to the previous invaders, the Vikings. They christened its mighty harbour *Vethrafjorthr* or 'the ford of Father Odin', Odin being a Norse god. Like its neighbour, Co. Kilkenny, to the north, Waterford was part of the kingdom of Ormond during the Middle Ages. Dating from far earlier in the county's history are a variety of passage tombs and graves, while the Neolithic dolmen at Knockeen is worth attention as the finest in Waterford. It boasts two capstones. Raising one stone, weighing a huge amount, would have been a tremendous achievement given the few resources of the Neolithic people. One wonders at the significance of those buried under these 'portal tombs'.

Far left: Tramore, one of the south coast's best-loved seaside resorts. The five-kilometre (three-mile) strand is one of its principal attractions.

Left: colourful yachts and other pleasure craft moored at the seaside resort of Dunmore East.

Below: imposing Lismore Castle, which dates from 1189, nestles amid thick deciduous forest on the banks of the River Blackwater.

Cork City

Right: the River Lee winds its way past the twin spires of St Finbarr's Cathedral. The river divides into two main channels in Cork, and the oldest part of the city stands on the section that lies between them. As Cork expanded it grew up the hillsides on either side of the river: a short but demanding walk up one of these hills will give a fine view of the city.

Below: Cork illuminated at night. The many watery reflections add a special atmosphere to this unique and enthralling metropolis.

The city of Cork has a fascinating history. Its name means 'marsh' and incredibly it is built on one, or at least on some dry land within the Great Marsh of Munster, through which runs the River Lee. It is impossible to cross the city without walking over several bridges, a unique aspect that gives it a special charm. Indeed, three of the city's finest streets – wide St Patrick's, the South Mall and the Grand Parade – actually span sheets of water, which in the eighteenth century were thoroughfares for ships.

The first construction within the marsh, however, was the seventh-century monastery of St Finbarr, which quickly grew to be an extensive and rich foundation. It was sited where St Finbarr's Cathedral (completed in 1870) stands today. A Viking trading settlement was made in the tenth century; later still the Anglo-Normans took the town. Numerous castles, churches and abbeys dating from this time have since disappeared as Cork became a thriving commercial centre; little remains from the sixteenth and seventeenth centuries either. Nineteenth-century buildings of note include the courthouse of 1835 and St Finbarr's Cathedral, the stained glass windows here being particularly fine Victorian examples of their kind.

Cork, the third largest city in Ireland, is known as a centre for agricultural produce, as well as distilling, ship-building, brewing and bacon-curing. It has a flourishing university and an informative museum in Fitzgerald Park, a gem of an attraction in the Crawford Municipal Art Gallery, which houses illuminating examples of Irish art from three centuries. There is also a plethora of great pubs, such as Dan Lowrey's Seafood Tavern on MacCurtain Street, where the fish pie is recommended.

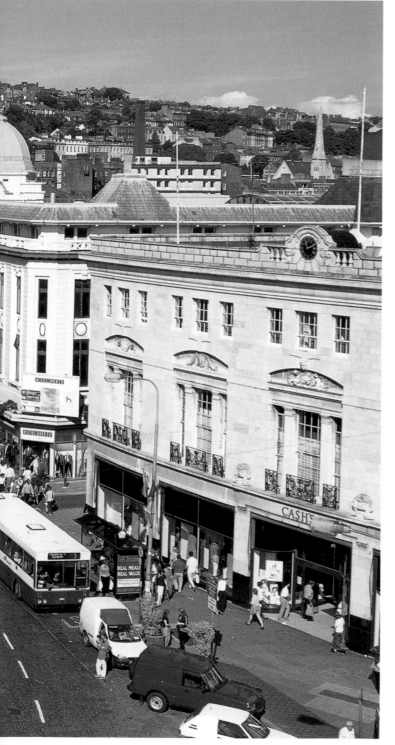

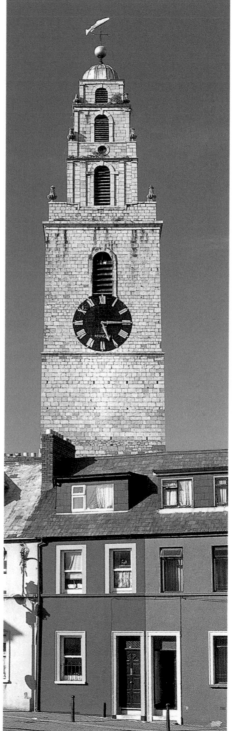

Far left: St Patrick's Street, one of Cork's best-known streets. At the head of the street stands a statue commemorating one Father Mathew, a nineteenth-century Temperance pioneer. The street is curved because it was built along and over a branch of the River Lee.

Left: the tower of St Anne's, Shandon, on the north side of the city. A Protestant parish church erected in 1722–6, St Anne's is famous for its bells: it contains eight and they are commended in Francis O'Mahony's well-known old song, 'The Bells of Shandon'. Members of the O'Mahony family are buried in a vault at the foot of the tower.

Above: a lively shopping street in Cork city. In contrast to its broad thoroughfares, Cork is also rich in narrow and more intimate streets that tempt the visitor with a range of intriguing small shops and quiet pubs.

Cork

The county of Cork is the largest county in Ireland and, as one might expect, is wonderfully varied in its scenery. Its most obvious features are the three main peninsulas to the west, and arguably the most picturesque locations are to be found in West Cork, renowned for its pretty villages, such as Kinsale, Baltimore and Schull, lying snug beside tranquil harbours, and country towns and hamlets, such as Bandon, Ballydehob and Glengarriff, set amid rolling hills. Here too are some superb beaches, such as that at Barley Cove. The bustling large town of Bantry is situated at the head of beautiful Bantry Bay.

The main attraction north of Cork city is the great Blarney Castle, which every visitor knows promises the 'gift of the gab', or eloquence, to all who kiss the stone at the top of the castle's tower. Blarney, built in 1446, is the most visited castle in Ireland.

To the east of the city lies the town of Cobh. For passengers arriving in Ireland on the Cork ferry, Cobh is the first town they see, just as it was the last of Ireland to be seen by thousands who emigrated to America in the latter part of the nineteenth century in the wake of the Great Famine. It was also the last port of call for the great transatlantic liners. The *Titanic* came here in April 1912; those disembarking, of course, were much luckier than they realised at the time. In those days the town was known as Queenstown, having been renamed in honour of Queen Victoria when she visited in 1849, but it returned to the older name – which means 'cove' – in 1922.

In the extreme east of the county, next to Co. Waterford, lies the popular resort and fishing port of Youghal, where the Elizabethan explorer and pirate Sir Walter Raleigh once lived.

Below: a solitary morning walker complements a serene study in blue near the seaside resort of Youghal.

Below: the lofty spire of St Colman's Cathedral dominates the town and harbour of Cobh. Built in the nineteenth century in Gothic style by the English architects Pugin and Ashlin, the cathedral is constructed of Dalkey granite and decorated with Irish marble.

Above: The Spaniard, a pub which lies high on Compass Hill in Kinsale. Low-ceilinged, thatched and friendly, this is one of the best-known pubs in Kinsale, frequented by poets, artists and music lovers, who come to enjoy the food and the live music.

Below: a cheerfully painted fishing boat moored at the harbourside in Kinsale. The narrow, winding streets offer a varied selection of shops.

One of the more famous and certainly well-loved of Cork's seaside resorts is Kinsale. Situated on the Bandon estuary on the slope of Compass Hill, the town only achieved prominence at the beginning of the seventeenth century. Then it was the location for several key events in Irish history. In 1601 a Spanish fleet arrived to assist the Irish against the English. Although surrounded by British forces, the Spanish held out until Irish help arrived overland and for a while the English were hard pressed on both sides. A lack of co-operation between the invading and rebelling forces eventually led to a significant, long-term Irish–Spanish defeat, however. Also the English king, James II, arrived in Ireland via Kinsale for his campaign to win back his throne from William of Orange. After his defeat a year later he was obliged to leave for the Continent from the same port.

Above: the battlements of Charles Fort, which lies just to the south of Kinsale. Remarkably well preserved, it is the largest fort in Ireland and dates from the 1680s. It was built to guard the town, whose vulnerability to attack had been proved at the turn of the seventeenth century.

Right: Summer Cove, Kinsale, a delightful seaside resort.

Below: the renowned unbroken crescent of sand at Barley Cove, West Cork. Bordered by unspoilt dunes and flanked by high hills, Barley Cove is the perfect destination for beach lovers. It offers much of interest to the enthusiastic ornithologist and naturalist.

SCHULL

Nestling at the foot of Mount Gabriel in West Cork, Schull is fast becoming a major tourist attraction. Long the haunt of artists attracted by the special quality of light and cloud shadows in Roaring Water Bay, Schull is now also renowned for its restaurants and pubs. It has a fine bookshop and an organic healthfood store – a sign of its sophisticated clientele, which includes visitors from all around the world – as well as the more traditional delights of sailing and swimming in the tranquil bay. The town can even boast Ireland's only planetarium. Walkers in the countryside around the town and up Mount Gabriel to the north are rewarded with magnificent views as far as the Fastnet Rock lighthouse in the distant Atlantic.

Above: gaily coloured shopfronts in Schull, West Cork. Although a small town consisting of just one main street, Schull has several antique shops, teashops, two supermarkets, three art galleries and a delicatessen – as well as numerous fine pubs and restaurants.

Above: an almost Mediterranean scene with sparkling blue seas and colourful houses at Glandore, West Cork, one of the county's most attractive villages.

Below: Drombeg Stone Circle, near Glandore. The shape of the circle, which dates from 2000 B.C., suggests it was used in sun worship.

West Cork is known for a considerable number of stone circles. The most famous is at Drombeg, near Glandore, east of Skibbereen. Here seventeen standing stones form a ring with a diameter of nine metres (thirty feet). One of the stones is horizontal, which is thought to be a deliberate construction, since a line through this stone to the entrance and beyond points to where the sun sets at winter solstice. The circle is thought to date from the Bronze Age, *c.* 2000 B.C. and have some ceremonial religious significance. Nearby lies a *fulachta fiadh* or 'deer roast', an ancient stone trough set by a stream that was used for boiling meat. Such sites, marked by blackened earth, are located all over Cork but are rarely uncovered, especially if the trough is absent.

The nearby hamlet of Glandore is a renowned beauty spot. Lying beside the River Leap as it enters the sea, Glandore is a little fishing village with simple, colourful houses and clear blue water. Like Glengarriff farther to the west, it has an extremely mild climate. Warmed by the Gulf Stream Glengarriff, is known for its lush vegetation. The glen is craggy and wooded, and most of the year is covered with flowering fuchsias and arbutus.

Above: tranquil, simple and complete: St Finbarr's Oratory stands on an island in the dramatic corrie lake of Gougane Barra near the Cork–Kerry border. St Finbarr built a hermitage on the island, reached by a causeway, before he founded a monastery at the mouth of the River Lee in Cork.

Left: a round of golf in the fairest of surroundings at Glengarriff, West Cork.

Blarney Castle is the strongest in Munster. The keep is built on a rock overlooking the river Martin and has withstood a number of sieges. The famous Blarney Stone is the bottom stone of the projecting battlements of the keep. Kissing it is less dangerous than it used to be; railings have been added to prevent the intrepid from falling to the ground should they slip, but even so one must hang head downwards to gain the gift of eloquence! Why the stone should be invested with such powers is a mystery, and probably a nineteenth-century invention rather than an ancient legend; nevertheless, the castle draws crowds all year round eager to give it a go.

Another major attraction in West Cork is Bantry House, which overlooks the spectacular panorama of Bantry Bay. Open to visitors, this Georgian stately home is famous for its art treasures, collected by the Earls of Bantry in the early nineteenth century. Among them are four Aubusson tapestries said to have been made for Queen Marie Antoinette. The sloping gardens and grounds of the house are Italianate in design, formal and exquisite.

Bantry Bay itself is broad, very deep and free from rocks, and has been the harbouring place of two invading French fleets. Neither fleet successfully landed, however. It affords the more peaceful visitor today some fine fishing. Nearby Garinish Island has gardens established by Harold Peto which have acquired an international reputation.

Left: a remote windswept smallholding overlooking surf-strewn rocks, and, in the distance, Cod's Head, near the Allihies towards the tip of the Beara Peninsula, West Cork.

Above: the Allihies, overlooking Ballydonegan Bay, on the Beara Peninsula, West Cork, an area populated in the nineteenth century by Cornish copper miners. They built a village whose remains can still be seen.

Kerry

Kerry is renowned as the most beautiful of all of Ireland's counties and receives thousands of visitors each year. The Ring of Kerry – a route through the highest mountains in Ireland – is world famous, as is the Dingle Peninsula's cliffs and shores, peaks and ports.

Although Tralee is the county town of Kerry, Killarney is the more frequently visited town owing its popularity to its proximity to Killarney National Park. The views of the mountains – Macgillycuddy's Reeks in particular – along the road from Killarney to Tralee are unsurpassed, their serrated edges silhouetted by the twilight on a summer's evening unforgettable. An international-standard golf course and superb fishing rivers are also on offer. The town's cathedral was designed by A.W. Pugin, and is one of his best in Ireland.

The three main loughs that comprise the best-known 'Lakes of Killarney' are impressive in their size and setting amid the mountains. Other fine lakes can be discovered on a variety of beautiful walks, or in the 'jaunting cars' – ponies and traps – that can be hired in town. Also worth visiting is Muckross House, an elegant stately home whose gardens are a delight, and whose interior houses a permanent exhibition of Kerry folk-life. Some rooms remain decorated in the style of its original era, giving an idea of nineteenth-century life.

Above: Lough Leane, near Killarney, is the largest of the famed Killarney Lakes. There are over thirty islands within it and a splendid waterfall, known as O'Sullivan's Cascade, can be seen on its cliffs.

Right: a colourful spring border beside Muckross House in Killarney National Park. The house, built in 1843, is one of the main attractions of the park.

THE SKELLIGS

Lying off the coast of Co. Kerry, the three dramatically rocky islands known as the Skelligs have a fascinating history. Skellig Michael, or Great Skellig, the largest of the three, is a huge rock rising to over two hundred metres (650 feet) above the sea, and is famous for its beehive huts. These are the remains of a deeply austere monastic order founded, it is thought, by St Finan in the seventh century. Built without mortar, these small, domed 'cells' have weathered the elements for over a thousand years, a tribute to the great skill of the monks who built them. Their situation out in the wild Atlantic cannot fail to emphasise the spiritual dedication and material indifference of the men who lived in them for five centuries.

Above: Little Skellig, a rocky promontory off the coast of Co. Kerry, a haven for breeding gannets of international importance, as seen from the walls of one of Great Skellig's beehive huts.

Above: a dog takes its ease outside a typical shop in Glenbeigh, a little seaside resort that has become a noted angling and golfing centre.

Left: the Valencia river at Cahersiveen. This little market town was the birthplace of the important nineteenth-century Irish politician, Daniel O'Connell, and the ruins of his house can be found just outside the town.

Left: the strand at Glenbeigh affords a fine view of the mountain of Seefin, some five hundred metres (1640 feet) high to the south.

Far left: a bicycle propped against a traditional stone cottage in Glenbeigh.

Above: a view of the Blasket Islands, in the Atlantic Ocean off Slea Head. Now uninhabited, the islands were once the home of several important writers in Irish.

Right: the harbour at Dingle. The 'most westerly town in Europe', Dingle is the perfect centre from which to explore the delights of the peninsula that bears its name.

The Dingle Peninsula is Co. Kerry's Atlantic jewel. It is dominated at its base by the magnificent peaks of the Slieve Mish mountain range, the highest summit of which – Baurtregaum – reaches 850 metres (2800 feet). Roads running to the north and south of these mountains afford superb marine and mountain views, particularly through Conor Pass en route to Dingle. From the road that descends into the town there is the wonderful sight of the mountains of the Iveragh peninsula across Dingle bay.

Dingle itself, snug at the foot of Ballysitteragh beside an almost perfectly enclosed harbour, is an exquisite fishing village. It was the site of a Celtic fort and during the Middle Ages was one of the western ports that traded with the Spanish. Around Ventry, another village a little further along the peninsula's southern coast, can be found over a hundred ancient remains, the most noteworthy being stone forts, clochauns and beehive huts. At the tip of the peninsula, towards the Blasket Islands, Gaelic is still the language of choice, and the locals are renowned for the special purity of their dialect.

Notable beauty spots include the road from Ventry round the end of the peninsula to Slea Head, with its vistas of surf-washed beaches and white cliffs, and the immaculate length of sand at Inch strand near Anascaul. In the north, Mount Brandon is famed for its dramatic landscape and Alpine flora.

Above: drystone walls and a carefully nurtured crop on a smallholding en route to Slea Head, at the tip of the Dingle Peninsula.

Left: Gallarus Oratory, a corbel-roofed, dry-masonry little church to be found south of Smerwick Harbour at the end of the Dingle Peninsula.

Far left: sunset over the Blasket Islands. Now abandoned, the islands were inhabited until the 1950s. They can be visited by boat from nearby Dunquin.

Limerick

S ome of the best pasturage in Ireland is to be found in Co. Limerick, in the heart of the province of Munster. Horses and cattle thrive on its level and rich central plain, bordered along its northwestern length by the Shannon River, and elsewhere by hills and mountains.

Limerick town was established as a Viking settlement in the tenth century and was subsequently enlarged by the Anglo-Normans a century later. They built King John's Castle in *c.* 1200, one of the finest examples of Anglo-Norman architecture in the country, which stands stalwart beside the Shannon. The castle is predated, however, by St Mary's Cathedral, which was founded in 1172 by one of the High Kings of Munster, Donal O'Brien. Although much changed since its original Romanesque form, the church has some interesting features, especially its black oak choir.

Limerick today is a busy seaport and a thriving agricultural and manufacturing centre, the fourth largest city in all of Ireland. In the eighteenth century the city walls were dismantled and broad streets of fine Georgian houses were built which lend the city an air of elegance and grace.

This page: the little village of Adare is known as the prettiest in Ireland and is famed for its cottages. Built by the Earl of Dunraven in the early part of last century, they look strikingly English.

Far left: Adare Manor, one of Ireland's most luxurious hotels. Originally built in the eighteenth century, its nineteenth-century 'Tudor Gothic' revisions now dominate its style.

Clare

Above and right: the Cliffs of Moher are an important haunt of a rich variety of seabirds, including kittiwakes, guillemots, razorbills, puffins, fulmars and shag.

Below: O'Brien's tower, atop the Cliffs of Moher, was built in the nineteenth century as a tea house.

Two unique features of County Clare are the Cliffs of Moher and the Burren. The cliffs are the most dramatic sea cliffs in Ireland, and possibly in Europe. Forming a sheer precipice from the waves to a height of 200 metres (660 feet), they extend for over eight kilometres (five miles). Their composition of shale and limestone gives alternating black and cream strata. Visitors walking the cliffs will find shale in the pasture beside them, blown by the savage winds up from the cliff face and over them, and sudden gusts are capable of toppling a person over the edge. During the last century a quaint castle-shaped tea house known as O'Brien's Tower was built close to the cliff edge. It no longer offers tea but on a clear day it affords excellent views of the cliffs and of the Aran Islands to the northwest.

The Burren is another of Clare's geological marvels. It comprises bare limestone terraces, riven with deep gullies and cracks, in which rare Alpine and Arctic flowers can be found. The area can seem bleak but the Burren in spring, when the unremitting stone pavements are splashed with brightly coloured flowers, is quite unique.

Clare is renowned for its music. May sees the return of *An Fleadh Nuea*, a festival of traditional music in Ennis, but 'singing' pubs reverberate all year round with the sounds of the fiddle and flute, the bodhrán and uillean pipes.

Below: A street scene in Lisdoonvarna, a town best known for its September folk festival. The highlight of the festival is its match-making aspect.

Clare is bordered by the Shannon estuary in the south, the Atlantic in the west and Galway Bay in the north, but the visitor tends to remember the county's seaside towns and villages: Ballyvaughan overlooking Galway Bay, Doolin with its internationally known old 'singing' pub, O'Connors, Lahinch, a popular golf and bathing resort with a superb strand on Liscannor Bay, Kilkee with its fabulous cliff scenery between Loop Head and Doonbeg, and Kilrush, a busy port on the Shannon.

Yet inland Clare villages and towns are just as interesting. In Victorian times, Lisdoonvarna, situated south of the Burren, was once Ireland's premier spa, with several distinct springs, each prescribed to cure a particular health problem. Today, although the spa still exists, the town's prescription is for merrymaking: its conviviality during its famous 'match-

making festival' that lasts all through September is nationally famous.

Ennistimon, directly to the south, is prettily sited on the Cullenagh river in a wooded valley and is a mecca for anglers. Ennis, the county town, to the southeast of Clare, still retains its narrow street plan dating from *c.* 1240 and the ruins of a Franciscan friary in its centre by the river Fergus.

Above: the River Cullenagh picturesquely cascades through the centre of Ennistimon, noted as the birthplace of the author Brian Merryman in *c.* 1747. He wrote the famed Gaelic poem, 'The Midnight Court'. The poem, which has often been translated into English, is a witty, heartfelt and amusing attack by Irish women on the sexual mores of their men.

Right: the romantic lone tower known as Doonnagore Castle overlooking the Atlantic near Doolin, is visible from the road from Doolin to Knockardin.

THE BURREN

This region has unique flora and fauna: certain types of fritillary butterflies, such as the pearl-bordered, can only be found here, and Arctic and Mediterranean flowers grow side by side as they do nowhere else in Ireland. The uplands are dry, but a warren of underground caves has been created by water seeping through the porous limestone. The most spectacular prehistoric site in the region, Poulnabrone Dolmen, a megalithic portal tomb, stands on raised ground in the Burren. Its long, flat, comparatively thin capstone balanced, seemingly lightly, on gently narrowing supports give it a special flair and grace, for all that each of the stone slabs weighs many tons. Excavations unearthed the bones of fourteen adults and six children, as well as pottery and stone artefacts, which date back to 2000–2500 B.C. Other sites in the Burren are Cahermore stone fort and the Gleninsheen wedge tomb.

Above: drystone walls of limestone on the Burren.

Left: Poulnabrone Dolmen, an image which has come to symbolise ancient Ireland in tourist brochures and media images the world over.

Left: a bicycle propped on a lamp-post awaits its owner in the Bunratty Folk Park. During the summer this re-created village is populated by actors in costume who perform the type of daily tasks that would have been the norm here at the turn of the century.

Right: Bunratty Castle, one of the country's greatest tourist attractions. The castle has been restored to look as it would have done in the sixteenth and seventeenth centuries. Mock medieval banquets are held where guests eat in style in the Main Guard room, waited upon by costumed serving men and women and entertained by music of the period. The castle's 'traditional Irish nights' are a big success too.

Left: McInerney & Sons, the immaculately re-created ironmongers on Bunratty's Main Street. The village also has eight farms, a watermill, a forge, a printers, a post office and a pub – all working as they would have been in the nineteenth century.

Above: a typically pretty cottage in the Bunratty Folk Park. The park consists of beautifully restored modest shops and cottages designed to show life in a typical Irish village at the turn of the century.

CONNACHT

Encompassing the mountains of Connemara, Mayo and Sligo, Connacht is the heart of 'romantic' Ireland.

Galway City

Galway is a lively city, the largest in the province, and a successful, developing centre for high-tech industries. Its position at the head of Galway Bay and the foot of mighty Lough Corrib made it an attractive trading post and it flourished under the Anglo-Normans' 'Fourteen Tribes of Galway' – fourteen main families who ran the city for the succeeding centuries, until Cromwell's time. After this it fell into decline, but the establishment of University College Galway, however, and increased urban and harbour renewal have improved the city's image and prospects, and today the future is bright.

Once a walled town, Galway has retained this sense of compactness and most of its sights are within easy reach. The town centre boasts the spectacular Quincentennial Fountain, which mimics the sails of a Galway hooker boat, the distinctive sailing boats which travelled Galway's Atlantic coast in the last century. The city's huge Cathedral of Our Lady Assumed into Heaven and St Nicholas was completed in 1965, and is thought to be the last great stone cathedral in Western Europe, its copper dome rising serenely above Galway's roofs, and its interior replete with marble and limestone. By way of contrast, the Collegiate Church of St Nicholas is the city's finest medieval building. Resplendent with finely carved gargoyles, it stands close to a sixteenth-century townhouse known as Lynch's Castle. Formerly the residence of the Lynches, one of the great merchant families of Galway, the castle is now a bank.

Previous pages: Roundstone harbour, Connemara, Co. Galway

Above: Galway's small and narrow streets are a mecca for shoppers looking for the unusual and interesting.

Left: the Salmon Weir, Galway city. In the winter months hundreds of salmon can be seen waiting in the River Corrib for the opportunity to swim upstream and spawn in Lough Corrib.

Below: Galway cathedral at night, reflected in the River Corrib. Designed by J. Robinson, the cathedral is built on an island site, formerly that of a prison.

Galway

Above: drystone walls surround painstakingly constructed fields on Inisheer Island, one of the Aran Islands. The islanders still 'make soil' in this otherwise barren landscape by combining seaweed and sand, which they gather by hand on the shore and bring to the 'field' by donkey.

Right: a sheer cliff face, typical of the scenery of the Aran Islands. St Enda founded a monastery here in 490 which over the centuries instructed many of Ireland's greatest saints, including Colmcille, Brendan and Colman.

Co. Galway, the second largest county in the country, is divided into east and west by Lough Corrib, a huge lake. The undisturbed beauties of Connemara, in Western Galway, with its high, lonely mountains and wild lakes and peatlands, perhaps epitomise the Irish landscape. Connemara has been called Europe's last great wilderness, for even today there are no towns or villages and few habitations of any sort in its heartland.

Eastern and southern Galway have lush pastures and historical sights ranging from the village of Aughrim, the site of the last great land battle on Irish soil, to the tower house of Thoor Ballylee, a 'castle' that belonged to Ireland's greatest poet, W. B. Yeats. He wrote some of his finest works under its roof. It is now open to the public.

In Galway Bay lie the Aran Islands: Inishmaan, Inisheer, and Inishmore, famed for an intriguing combination of austere landscape and rich cultural life. Irish is still spoken, and farming and fishing are the main sources of income (now supplemented by tourism). The islanders still wear traditional costume – a red flannel skirt and a shawl for the women, a sleeveless jacket for the men – and travel by currach, an open rowing boat, on the high seas.

Right: the stone fort known as Dun Aengus on Inishmore, one of the finest of its kind in Europe and definitely the most spectacularly sited.

Connemara, the wild and desolate region of western Galway, never seems crowded, for all that it attracts many hundreds of visitors each year. The main town, Clifden, is an excellent base for touring the region. It enjoys a wonderful setting by the sea with a beckoning view of the distant Twelve Bens and Connemara National Park to the east.

Dan O'Hara's Homestead and Connemara Heritage Centre lie just outside the town. This little farm is a re-creation of a modest nineteenth-century smallholding that was once typical of the area. It is centred upon the original house that belonged to one Dan O'Hara in pre-Famine days. Faced with the threat of starvation by his blighted potato crop, O'Hara abandoned his home and sailed to America in the 1840s. He was one of millions such Irish people, especially in the West, who were obliged to emigrate in the face of relentlessly bleak economic conditions. The severity of life on this subsistence farm is clear even today. The centre has also re-created the crannog, a rudimentary thatched house built on an artificial island in the middle of a lake. Crannogs originated during the Bronze Age, but a few remained in use even into the seventeenth century.

Connemara National Park lies at the heart of the region, and incorporates some of the peaks known as the Twelve Bens. It is home to herds of newly reintroduced red deer and a fine group of purebred Connemara ponies, some of which the visitor might be lucky enough to see. Also on view are numerous prehistoric remains: people have lived in this region for over 5000 years. At certain times of the year purple moor grass and flowering heather are visible on the mountain slopes, and closer examination will reveal orchids and bog asphodels, while numerous songbirds such as larks and robins may be heard.

Above: the humble abode of Dan O'Hara at the Connemara Heritage Centre, near Clifden, where life in pre-Famine Ireland has been re-created in all its austere simplicity.

Left: Connemara's largest town, Clifden, has a flourishing lobster-fishing industry and is known for its Connemara tweed. The wealth of craft shops in the town is indicative of the considerable artistic talent in the region.

Below: the thatched crannog featured at the Connemara Heritage Centre near Clifden. Crannogs were once a common sight in the lakes of Ireland.

Right: wild and lonely Aasleagh Falls, over which the Erriff River tumbles en route to Killary Harbour near the village of Leenane in northern Galway.

Below: Killary Harbour, whose northern shore is in Mayo, fringed by the Mweelrea Mountains. Its southern shore is in Galway alongside the peaks of the Maam Turk range. It is one of the most beautiful sea inlets on the west coast.

Right: rowing boats moored beside a small jetty where a mountain comes down to the shores of a lake in Connemara. As the presence of the boats suggests, fine angling is available here, as in so many places in this unspoilt county.

One of the great sights of the Connemara region is Kylemore Abbey, found en route from Letterfrack to Leenane in the north of the county. Today this Tudor Gothic pile is a girls' school run by Benedictine nuns, but for most of the century it was a convent. It was built as the private home of an English millionaire, Mitchell Henry, who gave it to his wife in 1866. Henry served as an MP in Ireland, but after the sudden death of his wife and daughter he sold the house. The abbey interior is now private, but a thriving craft centre on the site is worth a visit. Another Connemara sight not to be missed is Ballynahinch, with its wonderful lake and wooded river lying beneath the Twelve Bens. The lake provides exceptionally good fishing, and on an island stands the ancient castle of the Martins, the family who ruled the surrounding countryside in the Middle Ages.

Equally good fishing is to be had at Oughterard to the east on the shores of Lough Corrib. Indeed, the town is so famous as an anglers' resort that fishing folk flock here in early summer and autumn to catch salmon and trout, fly-fishing being particularly popular.

By way of contrast, directly to the east of Galway lies Athenry, a small town rich not so much in fish as in history. Established by the Anglo-Normans after 1235, the town can still boast a great amount of its defensive walls, including five towers and a town entrance known as North Gate. These were constructed to protect a great three-storeyed keep, now a well-preserved ruin recently re-roofed by the Office of Public Works.

Above: Ballynahinch Lake, fed by the Owenmore River in Connemara. Some of the best fishing in the county is to be had along these peaceful and unspoilt wooded shores.

Above: the remaining part of what must have once been a large and impressive high cross stands in the market square at Athenry. On one side it depicts Christ's crucifixion, on the other the Virgin and Child.

Far left: Kylemore Abbey, once the nineteenth-century home of a Galway MP but today an exclusive boarding school for girls run by Benedictine nuns.

Below: the church of the Franciscan friary in Athenry once held the remains of the Earls of Ulster and the chief Irish families of the West, but its medieval monuments were destroyed by Cromwell's troops in the late seventeenth century.

Mayo

Above: Croagh Patrick, the extinct volcano named after Ireland's patron saint, overlooks Clew Bay near Westport.

Far right: Clew Bay, a stretch of water outside Westport, is known for its islands. The warrior queen of the Middle Ages, Grace O'Malley, was said to have had her castle on Clare Island.

Below: the colourful streets of Westport. A great angling centre, this Georgian town has two fine churches and a well-preserved eighteenth-century mansion.

It is easy to get away from it all in Mayo, since this west-coast county is a far cry from the busy metropolis elsewhere. The largest town, Castlebar, has a population of only 6000, and the tourist centre of Westport on Clew Bay only half that. The county, one of the most beautiful in Ireland, stretches from Killary Harbour in the south to Killala Bay in the north. In between to the west, the long and varied Atlantic coastline effortlessly provides Blue Flag beaches and superb coastal walks.

Westport, a Georgian town on Clew Bay, is the jewel of the county. Set within sight of Croagh Patrick, Ireland's holiest mountain, it is elegantly laid out, with two beautiful churches from the last century, a broad avenue of trees lining the Carrowbeg River and a variety of intriguing shops. It also boasts Westport House, the home of the Marquess of Sligo. Built in the eighteenth century, it contains an historic collection of treasures, including Waterford glass, silverware, paintings and an ornate marble staircase. In the grounds is a small zoo, and boating and sailing facilities are available on the mansion's sizeable lake.

St Patrick is thought to have spent over a month praying and fasting at the peak of Croagh Patrick, and the mountain has been a centre of pilgrimage ever since. On the last Sunday in July, pilgrims walk in the saint's footsteps to the summit. Many walk barefoot, on a route that is far from easy, to atone for their sins, and attend Mass.

The view from the summit is inspiring. Ireland's largest island, Achill, can be seen. Achill has been attracting artists for over a century; the famous Irish artist Paul Henry spent ten years painting the island. The results have become synonymous in many people's minds with Irish landscape.

Right: views of the sea along the Atlantic Drive on the island of Achill, in west Co. Mayo. The drive, which follows a circle around the south of the island, passes the fifteenth-century tower of Kildownet, once a stronghold of warrior queen Grace O'Malley.

Right: Achill scenery, the type which has attracted artists and writers from all over Europe looking for peace, beauty and a place to work.

Left: Trawmore Strand, near the village of Keel on Achill Island, generally acknowledged as the finest beach in Ireland. It stretches for five kilometres (three miles) between two great stretches of cliffs: the Minawn Cliffs and the Cathedral Rocks. Both are best viewed by boat.

KNOCK

Over one million pilgrims come to Knock, Co. Mayo, each year to worship at Our Lady's Shrine, one of the great Marion shrines of the world. In 1879, fifteen people saw an apparition of the Blessed Virgin Mary against the gable wall of the Church of St John the Baptist. This wall is incorporated into the shrine building. The Basilica of Our Lady, Queen of Ireland was built nearby; it can accommodate 20,000 people. Numerous miracles of healing have been recorded at Knock, leading to an annual pilgrimage.

Right: an apparition of the Blessed Virgin Mary appeared in 1879 at the famous gable wall at Knock.
Far right: the Basilica of Our Lady, Queen of Ireland.

Roscommon

Roscommon is embraced on the east side by the Shannon and on the west side by the Suck, one of its major tributaries. In the south and east it is classic Shannonside country; in the northwest the land is really an extension of the Plains of Mayo; in the north around Boyle it adjoins the lakeland and drumlin country of Leitrim. Boyle is the largest town. It is the site of an important thirteenth-century Cistercian abbey, in a good state of repair. The town grew up around the abbey. Nearby, in the Rockingham Desmene, Lough Key Forest Park is one of the finest such facilities in Ireland, affording wonderful views of the lake and the Shannon. A little further away, near the tiny village of Keadue, is the grave of Turlough O'Carolan, blind harpist and last great composer in the old Gaelic tradition.

South of Boyle is Frenchpark, birthplace of Douglas Hyde; he was the founder of the Gaelic League, which began the restoration of the Irish language, and first president of the Republic of Ireland. A little further south again, at Rathcroghan or Cruachan, stands the ancient coronation stone of the pagan kings of Connacht.

Strokestown Park House, on the main Dublin road, was formerly the country home of the Mahon family, and is now superbly restored as a museum to commemorate the Great Famine (1845–52). This part of the country in particular suffered grievously from the effects of that great catastrophe.

At Roscommon town there is a fine castle and an abbey. Just west of Castlerea, Clonalis House is the ancestral home of The O'Conor Don, descended from the last Gaelic king of Ireland who was ousted by the Anglo-Normans in the 1270s. The family line remained unbroken from father to son for twenty-four generations, and in the twenty-fifth has passed to a nephew!

Far left: Lough Doo, one of a number of fine lakes in the north of Co. Roscommon known for their good fishing and unspoilt settings.

Below: Boyle Abbey, in the town of the same name. The abbey was founded by Maurice O'Duffy in 1161 and is associated with Ireland's other great Cistercian abbey at Mellifont, Co. Louth.

Leitrim

Co. Leitrim is divided by Lough Allen, the first major lake formed by the Shannon on its journey south. Most of the county is mountainous but the southern end is more like an extension of the south Ulster drumlin country, with low, rolling hills and small lakes.

A tiny sliver of Leitrim reaches the Atlantic coast. This anomaly arose because the Catholic Church in Ireland deemed that every bishop should have access to the open sea without the need to be beholden to a brother prelate! Thus the Leitrim county border follows an older diocesan one.

Inevitably, the county is dominated above all by the great river. The Shannon is already impressive at this point close to its source; further south it grows and eventually it and its tributaries drain one-fifth of the entire island.

Carrick-on-Shannon, the county's capital, lies on the Shannon and is a pleasant town, being renowned as a mecca for coarse anglers since the quality of the fishing in the area is of a very high standard. It is also popular as a major cruising centre with its own marina. In the south of the county, the tiny village of Dromod is a model of neatness and good order. The restored section of the old Cavan & Leitrim narrow gauge railway, complete with steam engine, can be seen here. In the north is Dromahair town, which was O'Rourke country in Gaelic days. The ruins of their stronghold, Breffni Castle, stand nearby. Beside them is Old Hall, built in 1626 by the Villiers family, the English adventurers who displaced the O'Rourkes. Another interesting planter house is Parkes Castle, beside Lough Gill, which dates from the same period.

In the mountainous northeast of the county, Manorhamilton town is a good centre from which to explore Glencar Lough and to the southwest, Lough Gill, which is partly in Co. Sligo. Manorhamilton is built on land granted to Sir Frederick Hamilton by Charles I. The ruins of the manor Hamilton built in 1638 can still be seen. One can drop down to the coast from here, keeping Lough Melvin on one's right and looking across it to Fermanagh on the far shore.

Sligo

H e was born in Dublin, but Ireland's greatest poet, W. B. Yeats, spent his childhood in Sligo and it is forever associated with him. For him it was 'the Land of Heart's Desire' and he chose to be buried in the churchyard where his grandfather had been vicar just outside Sligo town in Drumcliff. His works refer to the landscapes of Sligo in an unforgettable style. His poem 'The Lake Isle of Innisfree', about Lough Gill, is perhaps the most famous. Sligo town holds the Yeats Summer School each August in his honour. Many of the speakers are notable poets themselves.

Sligo's lakes and mountains are the focus of a number of forest parks with walking trails and superb views. Some have nature reserves, such as at Lissadell, where Lissadell House is open to the public in the summer. Hazelwood also boasts the Half Moon Bay Sculpture Trail. In contrast to the woods and loughs, the county's great bays offer superb, usually unpopulated, strands, such as those that sweep around the shore at Mullaghmore and Enniscrone.

Sligo town is picturesque and friendly. The town existed in Viking times and its narrow streets beside the Garavogue River date to the eighteenth century. There are the remains of Sligo 'Abbey', a Dominican friary rebuilt after a fire in the early fifteenth century. Sligo's impressive Museum and Art Gallery has some fine works by Ireland's most renowned painter, Jack B. Yeats, the brother of W. B. Yeats.

Above: the modern statue of W. B. Yeats that stands in Sligo town centre in honour of Ireland's greatest poet. The statue is covered by excerpts from his works.

Far left: Drumcliff churchyard, where the poet W. B. Yeats asked to be buried, in the shadow of Benbulben. His grave bears the words: 'Cast a cold eye on life, on death,/ Horseman pass by.'

Below: Benbulben, an unforgettable mountain to the north of Sligo town, whose distinctive shape dominates the landscape for miles.

Above: Rosses Point, a well-known holiday resort north of Sligo town. It offers a yacht club, a championship golf course and two very fine beaches, while the water here is ideal for sea angling and windsurfing.

Left: Classiebawn Castle is a highly romantic landmark at Mullaghmore. The castle was built in 1842 by the English prime minister Lord Palmerston.

Right: Glencar Lake. This lough is noted for its waterfall at the eastern end, which has an unbroken descent of fifteen metres (fifty feet).

ULSTER

The delights of Ulster range from the Giant's
Causeway to Lough Neagh, Ireland's largest lake.

Donegal

Previous pages: the Giant's Causeway, Co. Antrim.

Right: Loughross Beg Bay. The coast of Donegal has some of the least spoilt beaches in Europe. They are every bit as fine as those in the more famous and developed southwest.

Below: the harbour at Killybegs, a picturesque fishing village on Donegal Bay, which is also known for its carpet weaving. Their quality is recognised internationally and Donegal carpets can be found in stately homes around the world.

Donegal is the most northerly county on the island. Its farthest point, Malin Head, lies well to the north of Northern Ireland. In Gaelic times, this was the stronghold of the O'Donnell clan, and O'Donnell remains one of the most common surnames in the county to this day. Its original Gaelic name was *Tír Conaill*, the land of Conall, a mythic ancestor. This has been anglicised as Tyrconnell, but it is the later name *Dún na nGall*, the fortress of the stranger, which forms the basis for the modern Donegal. The county was 'planted' with English and Scots settlers as part of the Plantation of Ulster in the early seventeenth century.

Topographically, the county is characteristic of the Irish Atlantic seaboard in general. High coastal mountains, breathtaking marine views, deep glens and lakes make it distinctive in an Ulster context, but recognisably similar to Mayo, Galway and Kerry further south.

The border with Northern Ireland has cut the county off from its natural economic hinterland. However, it has benefited from the growth of tourism. It has long been a haven for people in Northern Ireland: many from as far away as Belfast have holiday homes in the county. The northwest coast is a *Gaeltacht* or Irish-speaking region, where the dialect spoken is closer to Scots Gaelic than that spoken in Galway or Kerry. This reflects the long historical associations between Donegal in particular, and Ulster in general, with the west of Scotland.

Finally, there are the people. It sounds a cliché, but they are different: laid back, relaxed, speaking in an accent so softly seductive you might imagine yourself in the South Seas rather than the North Atlantic. As they say in Donegal, take it easy!

Left: modest cottages of traditional design near Dungloe, in northern Donegal. Dungloe is the village at the heart of the Rosses, and is known for its superb fishing in nearby Lough Meela.

Below: fishing boats before Gweedore, on the river Clady in north Donegal. The village owes its existence to a nineteenth-century philanthropist who invested large sums to improve the lot of his tenants by building the church, the school and the post office.

Left: the rocky headland of the Rosses in north Donegal, one of the most beautiful regions of this unspoilt county, especially noteworthy for its innumerable lakes. The Rosses are part of the *Gaeltacht*, where Irish is the language of choice.

Above: Letterkenny, Donegal's largest town, at the head of Lough Swilly. It is visible for miles as you approach it from the east or south since it stands on a slope.

Far right: Fanad Head, northern Co. Donegal, where the beaches are totally unspoilt.

Letterkenny, at the head of Lough Swilly, is the other major town in the county after Donegal town. Situated on a slope straddling the Swilly river and with the ranges of the Sperrins and the Derryveagh mountains within sight, Letterkenny is the largest town in the county. Particularly noteworthy is the Cathedral of St Eunan, a nineteenth-century Gothic-style edifice noteworthy for its examples of distinctive Irish stained glass by Harry Clarke and Michael Healy, as well as its Celtic decorations and marble altar.

Letterkenny is the gateway to the Inishowen Peninsula, the most northerly part of Ireland, which lies between Lough Swilly and Lough Foyle and is a small world of its own. To the west of Lough Swilly, the Fanad Peninsula contains pretty villages such as Rathmullan.

In the heart of Donegal county, amid the Derryveagh mountains, Glenveagh National Park seems to encompass the essence of wild Donegal. And yet within the park stands, in magnificent grounds, a Victorian castle. Its cultivated spaces contrast with the wild, untamed countryside all about. A visit to Glenveagh is a 'must'. Finally, there is Tory, the most remote inhabited island off the Irish coast, where most of the islanders speak Gaelic. You can travel out there in summer; in winter it's best to stay on the mainland!

Londonderry

The official name of this city is Londonderry, reflecting its origins in the Plantation of Ulster, in which the city of London was a major investor. However, people on all sides of the community commonly speak of it simply as Derry.

The site of the city of Derry was originally a Columban monastic foundation. The word Derry comes from the Irish *Doire*, a wood. However, the modern city dates from Plantation times in the first decade of the seventeenth century. It was the last fortified walled city built in Europe and the walls have survived intact to this day. The original Plantation town was contained within the walls. It occupies a natural defensive site, sitting magnificently on a hill by a wide bend in the River Foyle.

The Church of Ireland Cathedral of St Columb dates from early Plantation days (1628–33) and stands at the highest point of the walled town. Just outside the walls, at the bottom of the steep Shipquay Street, stands the mock-Tudor Guildhall built in the 1880s. In the eighteenth century, the city spread beyond the confines of the walls: there are many fine Georgian town houses in William Street and Great James Street.

The north of the county is more fertile than the south. The other major town is Coleraine, about fifty kilometres (thirty miles) along the coast to the east of the city. It is a market town and an important university centre: the principal campus of the University of Ulster is nearby. Just over a mile south of Coleraine is Mount Sandel, the earliest known site of human habitation in Ireland. It dates from almost 6000 B.C.

Perhaps the most celebrated location in south Derry in modern times is the little village of Bellaghy, birthplace of Seamus Heaney, Ireland's most famous living poet and Nobel laureate.

Far left: part of Derry's famous city walls, in front of the Guildhall near Shipquay Gate. The walls, which date from 1618, are among the best preserved fortifications of their kind in Europe.

Below: traditional Irish dance performed by young girls wearing the distinctive embroidered costumes. All forms of traditional dance have enjoyed a recent revival in Ireland following the success of *Riverdance*.

Antrim

Above and right: the Giant's Causeway, on the north coast of Co. Antrim. At first sight, it is hard to believe that these smooth and regular columns were not made by human hands. It is estimated there are 37,000 columns in all, however, so it would have been quite a task for any sculptor!

The county of Antrim is a rare jewel. It is the most northeasterly county on the island and it is almost certain that the first inhabitants of Ireland travelled here from Scotland at the end of the Ice Age. You can see why if you drive along the magnificent Antrim coast road north from Larne to Ballycastle: the Mull of Kintyre is clearly visible across the sea, only twenty kilometres (thirteen miles) away at the narrowest point.

Along the way, the nine glens of Antrim – the finest of which are Glendun and Glenarmrun – run down to the coast. Just west of Fair Head, the town of Ballycastle plays host to the famous Oul Lammas fair every August and is the embarkation point for the ferry to nearby Rathlin Island. The north Antrim coast is distinguished by its numerous sea stacks; the most famous, at Carrick-a-rede, is joined to the mainland by a precipitous rope bridge. Don't cross it if you have a bad head for heights!

Between Carrick-a-rede and the seaside resort of Portrush lies the Giant's Causeway, one of the most famous sights in all Ireland. It consists of thousands of polygonal columns of basalt running out to sea and was famously – if wrongly – described by Dr Samuel Johnson as 'worth seeing, but not worth going to see'. Nearby, the little town of Bushmills is the site of Ireland's oldest distillery, founded in 1608. Near Portrush, the sixteenth-century Dunluce Castle, a fortress of the MacQuillans, dominates the coast.

Inland, the principal market town is Ballymena, a sturdy Plantation foundation. The southern end of the county lies on the shores of Lough Neagh, which is the largest lake in Ireland and the centre of a thriving eel-fishing industry.

Above and left: the daunting Carrick-a-rede rope bridge that joins a tiny island to the Antrim coast. The bridge bounces and swings as soon as one steps on it.

Far left: Ballintoy harbour on the north Antrim coast. Ballintoy is so pretty in the summer sunshine, it has been likened to an Aegean fishing village.

GLENS OF ANTRIM

There are nine glens in Antrim: Glenballyeamon; Glencorp; Glenarm; Glencloy; Glenariff; Glenaan; Glenshesk; Glentaise and Glendun. All are glacial coastal valleys, gouged out by the retreating ice at the end of the Ice Age. It's hard to imagine that now, looking at these magnificent glens opening onto the coast, with their patchwork quilt of fields carefully tended right up the highest point where cultivation is possible.

Above the glens stands the plateau of the Antrim uplands, an escarpment separating them from the Bann valley and other lowlands in the centre of the county. This area of high moorland makes a pleasing contrast with the rich glens below.

Above: the waterfalls of Glenariff, one of the finest of the nine glens of Antrim, in the east of the county. The glen contains a forest park which the English writer Thackeray described as 'Switzerland in miniature'.

Belfast, the capital of Northern Ireland, has a character all its own. Although its first stirrings as a settlement date from Plantation days, it only truly began to develop during the Industrial Revolution in the nineteenth century. It then grew at a phenomenal rate and by 1900 was the most populous city in Ireland and an industrial powerhouse of ship-building, engineering and textiles. In common with many such cities, its economic fortunes have receded in recent times.

It may be an industrial city but it is beautifully situated at the head of Belfast Lough and overlooked by Cave Hill on the landward side.

The fine City Hall (1906), stands on the site of the old eighteenth-century linen hall and is the most imposing building in the city, an impressive monument to urban self-possession dating from the city's glory days. Other buildings of note are Clifton House (1774), Queen's University (1849), an outstanding example of Victorian Tudor, and the Grand Opera House (1895), on the corner of Great Victoria Street and Glengall Street.

Above: the Victorian splendour of the Botanic Gardens. The Palm House was built in 1839 in a style of great elegance, and its curving glass and cast-iron make it one of the features of the gardens.

Below right: the Opera House at night, a recently refurbished stately Victorian pile and always a popular venue for a wide variety of entertainment.

Across from the Opera House stands the Crown Liquor Saloon, perhaps the finest example of a classic Victorian gin palace in the British Isles. The only pub in the UK owned by the National Trust, it is well worth a visit.

Belfast has been in the world's headlines in recent decades for all the wrong reasons. It has been the centre of Northern Ireland's troubles and is a city of two deeply divided communities. Even so, it has maintained its own dry good humour and never-say-die spirit through it all. Perhaps the marvellous new Waterfront Hall, the finest concert hall in Ireland, will stand as a symbol of better times to come, in what is hoped will be a new era of peace and prosperity.

Above: Queen's University in Belfast, the most significant of Northern Ireland's educational establishments. The university looks very similar to Magdalene College, Oxford.

Left: a panorama of Belfast at night, with the City Hall clearly visible in the foreground.

Down

Down is a county of contrasts. The northern part is remarkably self-contained and was almost untouched by all the years of the troubles. The middle of the county consists of a mixture of good rolling farmland and solid market towns such as Banbridge, which shade into the southern suburbs of Belfast and its adjoining dormitory towns. In south Down, the rising countryside is dominated by the austere beauty of the Mountains of Mourne.

The pretty town of Downpatrick is an ancient centre of settlement. Once known as *An Dún* (the fort), the county took its name from the Anglicised version of this name. Since the twelfth century it has been believed that St Patrick is buried in the churchyard of the cathedral Church of Ireland. A granite boulder marks the spot where the national saint supposedly rests. The cathedral itself is a nineteenth-century restoration which may incorporate some of the original medieval foundations.

Newcastle is the best place from which to explore the Mournes, especially if you follow the fine road to Warrenpoint and the important market town of Newry. Nearer to Belfast, the little village of Hillsborough is a Georgian gem. Nearby, Ballynahinch was the site of a decisive battle in 1798. The picturesque Ards Peninsula on the shores of Strangford Lough contains, among other wonders, the great Mount Stewart House. One of Ireland's finest country houses, it was the childhood home of Lord Castlereagh.

Above: night falls over Strangford Lough. The north half of this long lough is a national nature reserve.

Left: Mount Stewart House. It contains the finest painting of a horse in the world, *Hambletonian, Rubbing Down*, by George Stubbs. It is also renowned for its spectacular gardens.

Below: the marina at Bangor Harbour, a prosperous seaside resort known for its yachting clubs. By contrast, 1600 years ago it was the training ground for some of Ireland's greatest saints at Bangor Abbey.

THE MOURNES

The popular poet and songwriter Percy French wrote that 'the Mountains of Mourne sweep down to the sea' and he was surely right. These formidable mountains, which form a solid land barrier on Ulster's southern frontier, do seem to sweep right into the Irish Sea.

The highest peak is Slieve Donard at 852 metres (2796 feet). When one stands on the waterfront at Newcastle, Slieve Donard towers imposingly above you from, it seems, the bottom of the street, creating the illusion that the mountain is much higher. The Mournes are a paradise for hill walkers, from the Tollymore Forest Park through Silent Valley and the Spelga Pass.

Above: Newcastle's long beach is overlooked by a fine promenade, as popular today as it was last century, when it was built as a seaside resort.

Right: the Mournes, silhouetted in the light of a summer's morning. These mountains are the highest in Northern Ireland, and are dominated by Slieve Donard, which rises above the town of Newcastle. On a clear day, it is possible to see the hills of the English Lake District from its peak.

Armagh

The 'orchard of Ireland' has had a turbulent past which belies its tranquil inland beauty. It has been a microcosm of Northern Ireland's divided population. The north of the county is strongly unionist, the south nationalist, with the middle section fairly evenly divided. The Orange Order was founded near Portadown in 1795; to this day, the town of Portadown is one of the most volatile flashpoints in the province.

Ironically, the elegant Georgian town of Armagh is also the ecclesiastical capital of the whole island. The twin cathedrals of the Roman Catholic and Church of Ireland (Anglican) communions stand on adjoining hills. The town also houses a fine observatory and a planetarium. The Mall, originally a racecourse, is a particularly pleasing public space.

To the west of the town lies the large prehistoric earthwork known as Navan Fort, all that remains of the mythical Emain Macha, the royal seat of ancient Ulster according to the sagas. Armagh is an Anglicised corruption of the name Emain Macha.

South Armagh was one of the strongest IRA redoubts during the years of the troubles. Yet it is beautiful hill country with a long folk tradition of its own. Slieve Gullion is the dominant natural feature; it rises to 577 metres (1893 feet). The many drumlins, along with numerous lakes and watercourses, traditionally divided Ulster from the rest of Ireland.

Above: the carved 'Celtic head' to be found in the Protestant cathedral of St Patrick in Armagh city is thought to be an ancient idol.

Far left: the brooding presence of the prehistoric tumulus of Navan. This fort was once the site of Emain Macha, the legendary capital of Ulster.

Below: the tower of the Protestant cathedral of St Patrick and the spires of the Roman Catholic cathedral of the same name face one another in the city of Armagh.

Fermanagh

Above: exploring the Marble Arch cave system near Florence Court. The caves, cut by streams thousands of years ago, are lit to show their wondrous formations.

Fermanagh is the only one of the six counties of Northern Ireland that does not touch the shores of Lough Neagh. It does not need to, for in Upper and Lower Lough Erne it contains some of the most outstanding inland waterways in Ireland. Moreover, although the lakeshore parts of the county are naturally flat, much of the rest is quite hilly. In particular, this is true of the west and southwest of the county near the borders with Cavan, Sligo and Donegal.

The county town, Enniskillen, lies prettily between two channels of the River Erne just before it opens out into the broad expanse of the lower lough. It is a natural centre for water sports enthusiasts of all kinds. The opening of the nearby Ballyconnell canal to cruisers has linked the Erne and Shannon systems, so that one can cruise from here all the way south to Killaloe, Co. Clare.

Enniskillen was originally a fortified stronghold of the Gaelic Maguires, but they were dispossessed in the early seventeenth century; the castle retains vestiges of the Maguire stronghold.

The Upper and Lower Lough Erne are both extremely rewarding. The remains of St Molaise's sixth-century monastery, including a fine round tower, can be found on Devenish Island. Boa Island is famous for its celebrated Janus head and White Island also contains interesting antiquities.

To the east of Enniskillen, near Portora school (where Oscar Wilde was once a pupil) stands Castle Coole, considered by many the finest country house in Ireland. To the southwest, in the area of the upper lake, Florence Court is less spectacular, although still impressive. Nearby, the Marble Arch cave system can be explored by boat, although this is not an activity for the faint-hearted!

Above: the River Erne at Enniskillen is guarded by the town's fifteenth-century castle.

Right: the famous and mysterious Janus Stone that stands in a Christian cemetery on Boa Island in Lower Lough Erne.

Tyrone

Tyrone, from the Irish *Tír Eoghan*, or the land of Eoghan or Owen, was the ancestral heartland of the O'Neills, the greatest family of Gaelic Ireland until their final defeat by the English in 1601. Their capital was at Dungannon, still an important market town in the middle of the county.

The modern county, the largest in Northern Ireland, is one of gently rolling hills and good land, except for the north near the Co. Derry border, where the Sperrin Mountains rise to 683 metres (2241 feet) at Sawel, the highest point. Tyrone has a long shoreline on Lough Neagh, the largest inland sheet of water in Ireland, and the area along the lough is naturally low-lying.

The county town, on the main Dublin to Derry road, is Omagh, a pleasant market town which was the scene of the worst – and it was hoped the last – terrorist outrage of the troubles in the summer of 1998. Set where the rivers Camowen and Drumragh meet to form the Strule, there are salmon leap 'stairs' to be seen and good fishing to be had here. Among Omagh's more famous sons is the playwright Brian Friel and the popular songwriter Jimmy Kennedy, who wrote 'Red Sails in the Sunset', among other ballads.

Just to the north of Omagh, the Ulster-American Folk Park is a major tourist attraction of reconstructed cottages, a farm museum, an audio-visual theatre and several exhibition galleries. Endowed by the Mellons, an American banking family, and featuring the 'ancestral homestead' from which Thomas Mellon emigrated in 1818, the park's most interesting aspect is its collection of reconstructed houses, which make clear the similarities and differences between the homes of eighteenth-century rural Ulstermen in Ireland and the dwellings they built as pioneer American emigrants. The contribution of these Ulstermen to the history of the United States was out of all proportion to their numbers. Many of them were Presbyterians, fleeing the vexatious rule of the then Anglican establishment. Their progeny, known as Ulster Scots in America, have produced numerous presidents and other notable figures in the history of the republic.

Left: the River Strule and Bell's Bridge, Omagh. The river is noted for its freshwater pearls. Omagh, the county town of Tyrone, is dominated by its cathedral, built in 1899, whose two unequal spires can be seen for many miles.

Monaghan

The county of Monaghan lies in south Ulster near the Leinster border. This is classic drumlin country, the low rounded hills rolling away to the horizon in every direction. The contrast with the plains of Leinster to the south or even with the much flatter land of mid-Tyrone to the north is very marked. These drumlins formed an effective barrier to the south Ulster approaches in the days before modern roads. They ensured that Ulster remained a secure Gaelic fastness until Elizabethan times. Even then, Ulster was only conquered with great difficulty, as the terrain made defensive ambush battles easy to stage and win.

This is not glamorous country. Its most famous son, the poet Patrick Kavanagh, who hailed from Inniskeen, a small village in east Monaghan, referred to its 'stony, grey soil'. This impression is misleading, however. Although not oustandingly good farming land (Kavanagh was a farmer's son), it is extremely pretty. The rolling drumlins, with their patchwork quilt pattern of fields, see to that.

There are only four towns of any consequence: Clones (pronounced Cloeness); Monaghan; Castleblayney and Carrickmacross, of which the latter is celebrated for its lace manufacture.

Ireland's most celebrated artists' retreat is at Annaghmakerrig, the former home of the theatre producer Tyrone Guthrie. This is also the home town of Patrick McCabe, author of the remarkable novel *Butcher Boy*.

Cavan

avan is lakeland: Lough Sheelin and Lough Ramor are situated in the south; Lough Oughter and the connections into the Upper Erne system are in the northwest near the Fermanagh border; Lough Sillan is in the northeast, near Shercock. In addition to these loughs, a multitude of smaller lakes are dotted across this area, one of the most unjustly neglected counties in Ireland.

As this might suggest, most of the county is flat except for the farthest northwest corner near Fermanagh and Leitrim, where the mountains rise quite steeply. The highest point, Cuilcagh, is 668 metres (2,192 feet). The Shannon rises on its slopes at a point known as the Shannon Pot, which is generally held to be the source of this great river.

The towns in Co. Cavan are small, many of them little more than big villages by European standards. Yet this is a paradise for anglers and water-sports enthusiasts of every kind. There is much history here too: this was the ancestral land of the O'Reillys, a powerful family in former Gaelic days. Shantemon Hill, near Cavan town, was the traditional inauguration site of the O'Reilly chiefs. The ruins of Clough Oughter Castle, a medieval O'Reilly stronghold, survive on an island in Lough Oughter.

The ruins of the Columban foundation at Drumlane, near Belturbet, include a medieval church and partially preserved round tower.

Left: the swollen River Erne rushes by Belturbet, a busy market town. The Ulster Canal started here and connected towns in Northern Ireland with those in the Republic.

Below: Drumlane ruins, the site of a sixth-century monastery founded by St Maedoc, a pupil of St David of Wales. A distinctive round tower on the site is of particular interest.